They Took the Children

by David Hollinsworth

working title press

DEDICATION
To Carol Kendall

The children's illustrations and quotations that appear throughout this book were done by students of St Peter's Lutheran School, Blackwood, for SA Link-Up, as part of Reconciliation Week and National Sorry Day 2000. SA Link-Up is a program of Nunkuwarrin Yunti of South Australia Inc.

LEXILE™950

Working Title Press
ABN 29 076 867 751
33 Balham Avenue
Kingswood SA 5062
www.workingtitlepress.com.au

First published 2003
Reprinted 2007

Text copyright © David Hollinsworth 2003
Copyright in the individual images in this book remains with the copyright holders as acknowledged.

Designed and set in New Aster and Helvetica by Patricia Howes
Printed in Singapore by Tien Wah Press (Pte) Ltd

All rights reserved. No part of this publication may be reproduced or transmitted in any form or by any means, electronic or mechanical, including photocopying, recording, storage in an information retrieval system, or otherwise, without prior written permission of the publisher, unless specifically permitted under the *Copyright Act 1968* as amended.

National Library of Australia Cataloguing-in-Publication entry

Hollinsworth, D. (David).
They took the children.

For primary school students.
ISBN 978 1 876288 13 6.

1. Aborigines, Australian – Children – Juvenile literature.
2. Aborigines, Australian – Removal – Juvenile literature.
3. Aborigines, Australian – Government policy – Juvenile literature.
4. Aborigines, Australian – History – Juvenile literature. I. Title.

362.849915

Why me; why was I taken? It's like a hole in your heart that can never heal.

It's like you're the first human being at times. You know, you've just come out of nowhere; there you are. In terms of having a direction in life, how do you know where you're going if you don't know where you've come from?

From the *Bringing Them Home* report.

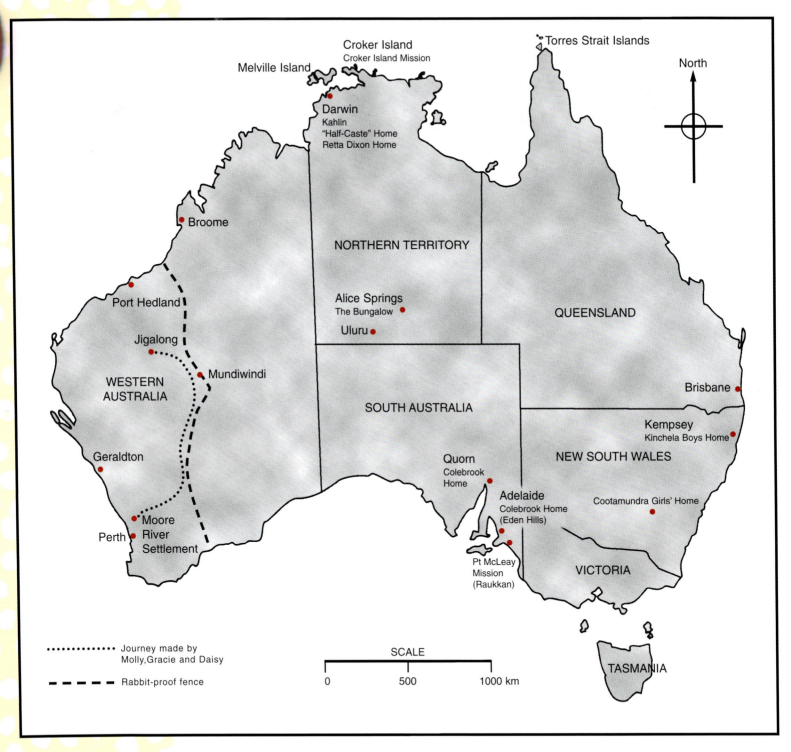

Map showing some of the settlements and institutions where Aboriginal children of the stolen generations grew up. Also shown is the journey of Molly Craig and her cousins, Daisy and Gracie, along the rabbit-proof fence.

Introduction

In 1930 three Aboriginal girls, Molly aged fourteen, her cousin Gracie aged eleven and her sister Daisy aged eight, were taken from their mothers by Western Australian police.

They were sent thousands of kilometres south to a children's home on the Moore River Settlement, north of Perth.

The children ran away and for many months hid from the police who chased them. They walked back home by following the fence that had been built to stop rabbits moving into farming land. (See map opposite.) The fence went north for 2,400 kilometres, back to Molly's mother at Jigalong station.

Gracie was caught and returned to Moore River. When Molly and Daisy finally made it back to Jigalong, they stayed away from the police. Many years later when Molly had two daughters of her own, she was taken to hospital in Perth with appendicitis. As soon as she was well enough to travel, Molly was sent back to Moore River with her children.

The story of the amazing journey of these three children was told by Molly Craig's daughter, Doris Pilkington Garimara, in a book called *Follow the Rabbit-Proof Fence*. It was later made into a film, *Rabbit-Proof Fence*. You may have seen it.

The policeman came and took us, Gracie, Daisy and me, Molly. They put us in that place. They told us we had no mothers. I knew they were wrong. We run away. Long way from there. We knew we find that fence, we go home.

Molly Craig

Looking for the fence.
A scene from the film
Rabbit-Proof Fence.

Sadly, as this book will show, *Follow the Rabbit-Proof Fence* is one of many stories about thousands of children who were taken away from their Aboriginal parents.

These people are called the stolen generations. The account of the stolen generations is an unhappy one. But it is important for us to know what happened so that we can understand our history and work towards reconciliation.

Every Aboriginal family has been affected by these removals. Even if their own children were not taken, families were still frightened of what might happen. All of them knew nieces and nephews or other relatives who had not been so lucky.

Some of the children who were taken away came home, but many never saw their families again.

Non-Aboriginal people took the babies away. The Aboriginal Mums were sad. The babies did not want to be taken away.

William

The First Removals of Children

Settlers
People who came to Australia to live were called settlers.

Racism
Believing that people are inferior on the basis of the colour of their skin, their way of life or their religion is called racism.

Protector
The Protector worked for the government and was supposed to help Aboriginal people by giving them food and preventing the settlers from harming them.

The British settlers who came to New South Wales and the other colonies after the arrival of the First Fleet in 1788, thought they were right to claim the new land. They believed that their way of living and their beliefs were better than those of the Aboriginal people. Many of them wanted Aboriginal people to change to become more like them.

These people thought that it would be much easier to change the behaviour of children than that of adults.

Matthew Moorhouse, the Protector of Aborigines in South Australia, said in 1842: "Our chief hope is decidedly in the children; and the complete success as far as regards their education and civilisation would be before us, if it were possible to remove them from the influence of their parents".

From the beginning of the colony at Sydney Cove, individual Aboriginal children were taken into the homes of some settlers for education and training. Some of these children were taken after their parents died. Some were left by their parents in the care of settlers. Most of these children became lonely and ran away to join their families or died from disease.

In 1814 the Governor of the colony, Lachlan Macquarie, set up a boarding school for Aboriginal children at Parramatta in Sydney. It was intended that the children were to be given Christian religious instruction and training as servants. The headmaster, William Shelley, noted that the children learnt well but often wanted to join their parents. Shelley said that "the chief difficulty was the separation of the children from their parents". The school was closed in 1820 after all the students had run away to rejoin their families.

We at the government want to take that baby to school please. The Aboriginal family said "No, No, No, I don't want you to take them away." But they took them anyway. The Mum and the Dad felt sad – very sad.

Tori

Dispossession

As settlement spread out across Australia, and the number of settlers and their animals increased, clashes between the new and original inhabitants occurred over land and food and sometimes over women and children. Eventually the settlers, backed up by the police, overcame Aboriginal resistance.

Children who survived these fights were often taken to be servants. Some settlers seemed to think of these children as pets.

Missions and Reserves

Missions and reserves were places where Aboriginal people were sent to prevent them from mixing with settlers. If these places were run by church people, they were called missions. If they were run by the government or the police, they were called reserves.

In 1842, the artist Thomas Bock painted this picture of a young Aboriginal girl, Mathinna, at Government House in Hobart. Mathinna was five when she was taken by the wife of the Governor of Tasmania. She was later abandoned when they returned to England.

Aboriginal people who had lived on their land for more than 40,000 years were forced to work for the settlers or move to missions and government stations where they were issued with clothes and rations. Poor food, unsanitary conditions and new diseases meant that many Aboriginal people died.

At the same time that Aboriginal people were dying, more and more immigrants were coming to live in Australia. The drop in the number of Aboriginal people led most settlers to accept that Aborigines were going to die out completely. To protect them, it was decided to keep them separate from everyone else on missions or reserves.

These cartoons of the late nineteenth and early twentieth centuries illustrate the public opinion of the times — that Aborigines were inferior and doomed to die out completely.

(*Left*) "A Curiosity in her own Country" by Phil May, *The Bulletin*, 1888.

(*Right*) "Getting Near" by Glover, *The Bulletin*, 1927.

Protection Laws

Governments passed laws that took away the rights of Aboriginal people. The government (or the police) could make Aboriginal people leave or stay in a particular place, and could stop them from marrying, or working, or owning a home.

These laws (called Protection laws) also gave the government control of the children of any Aboriginal people. Government officials could take away the children of Aboriginal people regardless of what the parents and children wanted. They could put them in children's homes or, when they were about twelve years old, they could send them to work for the settlers.

On many of the missions children were forced to live in locked dormitories, which meant that while they still lived near their parents, they rarely had much contact with them. The missionaries became their parents.

In other instances, children were sent to orphanages or special homes far away where their families couldn't visit them.

Dormitories
Dormitories were large buildings where many children slept together. Boys and girls were often separated.

The one thing that really, really sticks in my mind is being put into this cold bed with white cold starchy sheets and having to sleep on my own and looking down the room and just seeing rows of beds and not knowing where my brothers and sisters were.

From the *Bringing Them Home* report.

Point McLeay Mission staff and children pose outside the mission buildings and church c.1885. The mission, or Raukkan as it is now called, was established on a traditional Ngarrindjeri site on the shores of Lake Alexandrina in South Australia in 1859.

Point McLeay school boys, c. 1880.

Classroom,
Point McLeay, 1927.

Young girls skipping
at Point McLeay
Mission School, 1930.

Toothbrush drill at Point McLeay.

Taking the Children Away

White or Black?
As British and European people moved around the world, they met people who looked different and who had other languages and ways of living. Some of these people had different coloured skin (black or yellow or brown). These colours came to stand for different races.

Many of the new settlers who came to Australia thought that because they were white they were better than the black Indigenous people. These people were upset and confused by the idea of a child with a white and a black parent. They were unsure whether to treat them as members of their own race or another.

Many children of Aboriginal mothers had white fathers. Some of the fathers wanted to keep the children but others didn't want to be responsible for them. These children were called "half-caste" as they were thought of as "half-black" and "half-white". As settlement increased, so too did the number of these children.

While it was expected that Aboriginal people would die out, the increase in so-called "half-castes" was considered to be another matter. In 1937 A. O. Neville, Chief Protector in Western Australia, asked at the national conference of State and Commonwealth Aboriginal Affairs ministers: "Are we going to have a population of one million blacks in the Commonwealth or are we going to merge them into our white community and eventually forget that there were any Aborigines in Australia?"

Many white people were angry that children who were nearly white were living with Aboriginal people. They thought that if these children were taken away and educated they could become like other white children. But for this plan to work, it was believed that the children would have to stop seeing their Aboriginal families.

> COMMONWEALTH OF AUSTRALIA.
>
> NORTHERN TERRITORY MEDICAL SERVICE,
>
> DARWIN, 7th. February 1933.
>
> His Honour,
> The Administrator of the
> Northern Territory,
> DARWIN.
>
> PERMISSION TO MARRY ABORIGINALS.
>
> With further reference to previous memoranda in which I have called attention to the very grave problem which has been developing in Northern Australia owing to the intermarriage of alien coloured races with aboriginals and half-castes, it is strongly recommended that the Commonwealth take action to have the States, particularly Queensland and Western Australia, adopt a policy uniform with that of the Commonwealth.
>
> For years it seems that Protectors of Aboriginals have regarded it as undesirable that a half-caste or quarter-caste aboriginal should be mated with a white. On the other hand mating with Japanese, South-Sea Islanders, Chinese and hybrid coloured aliens has been regarded as a very desirable solution to what was regarded as the marriage problem of coloured girls some of whom had over seventy-five per cent white blood. The result has been the accumulation of a hybrid coloured population of very low order. I am unable to speak for Western Australia and Queensland but these coloured individuals constitute a perennial economic and social problem in the Northern Territory and their multiplication throughout the north of the continent is likely to be attended by very grave consequences to Australia as a nation.
>
> In the Territory the mating of aboriginals with any person other than an aboriginal is prohibited. The mating of coloured aliens with any female of part aboriginal blood is also prohibited. Every endeavour is being made to breed out the colour by elevating female half-castes to white standard with a view to their absorption by mating into the white population. The adoption of a similar policy throughout the Commonwealth is, in my opinion, a matter of vital importance.
>
> (C.E. Cook).
> Chief Protector of Aboriginals.

A letter from the Chief Protector of Aboriginals, Dr Cecil Cook, in 1933, outlining his plan to eliminate "the hybrid coloured population" by preventing intermarriage between Asians and Aborigines, and to "breed out the colour".

The government said to the Mum, would your child like to come with me for a ride in the car with me. It was a trick. They took them far away, so the Aboriginal people could not see the babies again. They were sad.

Katherine

Under the law, the government could only take children away from their parents if they could prove that they were neglected or badly treated.

Some white children were also put into homes when it was demonstrated that their parents could not take care of them.

But for most children with an Aboriginal parent, little or no proof of neglect was required. The fact that they lived an Aboriginal way of life was seen by many government officials as reason enough to remove them.

It was assumed that these children would be much better off being taken away and raised to be white because the white way of life was seen as better. The people who took these children said it was "for their own good".

The policy of removing Aboriginal children and raising them to be like white people was part of the Assimilation policy. The Assimilation policy was intended to make Aborigines the same as other white Australians in terms of how they lived, what they did and what they believed. Its purpose was to prevent Aboriginal people from being different, or in other words, to stop them from being Aboriginal.

"State children". (*Top* and *Bottom*) Aboriginal children committed to the care of the State Children's Council, South Australia, c. 1911.

Down a Hole

Many Aboriginal mothers hid their children to stop them being taken away. Some were hidden in holes in the ground or caves when the police came. Sometimes light-skinned children were covered in ash or dirt because the police often left the dark children with their families.

Many families tried to hide or kept moving around to avoid the police. Molly Craig was fourteen years old when she was finally taken to the Moore River Settlement in Western Australia.

A scene from *Rabbit-Proof Fence*. Molly, Gracie and Daisy on their way to Moore River Settlement.

Parents who tried to stop their children being taken away could be put in gaol or made to leave their homes. Some parents wrote letters asking for their children to be returned.

Some police and other white people who witnessed the distress of these families, or who felt it was bad to take the children from their mothers, chose to ignore the government policy.

Sometimes, Aboriginal parents who were having trouble taking care of their children, agreed to let their children go away for schooling because they believed they would be better off with a good education. Many parents were told this decision was for the best.

Aboriginal people had a baby but they couldn't find their baby. Aboriginal people could not find their Mums and Dads. They were so sad when they got taken away.

Isabelle

A letter written by William Bray to the Protector of Aboriginals in 1941, requesting that his children be allowed to stay in Central Australia, where they were residents of the government-run institution, the Bungalow, in Alice Springs. By 1942 the Bungalow was closed and most of its children sent far away to missions on Melville and Croker Islands. (See map on page 2.)

> Protector Aboriginals.
> Alice Springs
> Central Australia N.T.
> April 1941
>
> Dear Sir.
>
> I myself, and my wife, both half castes we understand, do not want any of our children removed, out of this Central Australia their country.
>
> It would not be fair to us, the loss of them. Also not fair to them the loss of their parents, causing crying and fretting.
>
> We parents, born Arltunga goldfields. Children also, except one, he being the eldest, Norman. He born Deep Well, part of the east-west running James Range.
>
> As we were all born here in Central Australia, we don't know any other parts, and don't want to.
>
> Will you please place this Protest, as we do not understand any forcible removal, of any of us, from this Central Australia, our birthright country.
>
> Yours truly. W Bray.
>
> W. BRAY - His Signature

In the Children's Homes

Some children were taken as babies and never knew their parents. Others were of school age and some were teenagers. Those who were taken very young didn't know where they came from or who their family was. Those who had grown up with their families, like Molly Craig, often tried to run away to get back home. Most were caught and taken back.

Other children became used to the life in these homes. If the staff were kind, they became like parents for the children. But some of the staff were cruel or unfriendly. Often it was left to the bigger children to do the mothering of the younger ones.

Children in these homes were told to speak English, and were not allowed to use their own Aboriginal languages.

The food was poor and monotonous, and on many occasions the children went hungry. There were rarely any books to read or toys to play with. Children were often punished and sometimes beaten or locked up for disobedience.

Occasionally, brothers and sisters were kept together. But many were separated. People who grew up in these places say that all the children they lived with became like brothers and sisters because they never saw anyone else.

It's a wonder we all survived with the food we got. For breakfast we got a bit of porridge with saccharin in it and a cup of tea. The porridge was always dry as a bone. Lunch was a plate of soup made out of bones, sheep's head and things like that, no vegetables. For dinner we had a slice of bread with jam and a cup of tea. After dinner we were locked up in a dormitory for the night.

From the *Bringing Them Home* report.

I remember this woman saying to me, "Your mother's dead, you've got no mother now. That's why you're here with us". Then about two years after that my mother and my mother's sisters all came to the Bungalow but they weren't allowed to visit us because they were black. They had to sneak around onto the hills. Each mother was picking out which they think was their children. And this other girl said, "Your mother up there". And because they told me that she was dead, I said, "No, that's not my mother. I haven't got a black mother".

From the *Bringing Them Home* report.

Some children were told their mothers were dead or didn't want them. Some grew up not knowing they had Aboriginal relatives. Others thought they had no family at all. Those who could remember their families were instructed to forget about them. Many were told that Aborigines were bad or dangerous and that it was best to keep away from them.

Several of the children remember running away from the strange dark people who stared at them through the fence of the home. These strangers were their family but they didn't know it. Others saw parents, who may have spent months or years trying to find their children, being arrested in front of their eyes and removed from the area.

Some children who grew up in these homes were grateful. They thought it was better for them to get an education and stop living an Aboriginal way of life. Others disagreed violently with this point of view.

Meal time at Kahlin "Half-Caste" Home, Darwin, in the 1930s.

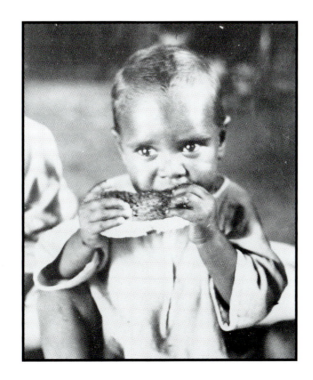

Meal time at the Bungalow, Alice Springs, 1928.

A publicity shot taken at Croker Island Mission in 1956 to advertise the success of the Assimilation policy overseas.

Kinchela Boys Home at Kempsey in New South Wales c. 1959.

Fostering and Adoptions

As more and more children were taken away from their families, the government found new ways of assimilating the so-called "half-caste" children.

Instead of putting lots of children together in big orphanages and homes, it was decided that one or two children should be placed with white families. The idea behind this was that if the children were brought up by families it might be easier for them to forget about their Aboriginal relatives.

We was bought like a market. We was all lined up in white dresses, and they'd come round and pick you out like you was for sale.

From the *Bringing Them Home* report.

"Adopted children", Retta Dixon Home, Darwin, c.1961

All the teachings that we received from our (foster) family when we were little, that black people were bad ... I wanted my skin to be white.

From the *Bringing Them Home* report.

Many children were adopted, which meant that their Aboriginal mother and father lost their rights to be parents, and the children were legally the children of the new parents. Under adoption laws, their names could be changed and the adoptive parents could refuse to let their birth parents see them. The government could prevent the Aboriginal family from finding out where the adopted children were or anything about them. For many parents it felt as if their children had died.

If Aboriginal parents refused to agree to adoption, government authorities could arrange for the children to be fostered. This meant that the children could be cared for by a white family, on the understanding that they might one day go home to their Aboriginal family.

Many children were adopted when they were very young. Some were only days old. Often these children grew up not knowing anything about their Aboriginal family. A lot of them were not even told that they had been adopted.

Some of the parents who adopted Aboriginal children were told wrongly that the children were orphans. Others were instructed to tell the children they were from overseas.

When these children finally found out the truth, it was an enormous shock to them.

This photo of children from the Kahlin "Half-Caste" Home in Darwin was used by the Minister of the Interior in 1934 to advertise in the southern states for foster homes for children from Kahlin and the Bungalow in Alice Springs.

After the photo appeared in the Melbourne *Herald*, a woman responded to the minister by offering to take "the little girl in centre of group" or "any of the others … as long as they are strong". She marked the photo with an X to indicate the girl she wanted.

Getting the Children Back

Throughout history, Aboriginal families tried to prevent the removal of their children whenever they could. In the early days of settlement, adults were sometimes killed when trying to stop their children from being taken.

Under laws that were introduced in the second half of the nineteenth and for much of the twentieth century, parents lost the right to control their children, and it became the responsibility of State governments.

Aboriginal people tried to change these government policies. In 1927 Aboriginal activist, Fred Maynard, from the Aborigines' Progressive Association, wrote to the Premier of New South Wales demanding "that the family life of Aboriginal people shall be held sacred and free from invasion and interference and that the children shall be left in the control of their parents".

Throughout the 1960s and 1970s Aboriginal people protested strongly against the Assimilation policies that attempted to make Aborigines abandon their culture and lifestyles. They wanted their culture to be respected. They wanted their rights to land

The baby was very sad and when she grew up she looked and she looked and she looked and she looked but she couldn't find her Mummy and Daddy. She wants to see her Mummy and Daddy but she didn't know that they died. She was sad.

Shannon

recognised. They wanted to receive the same help and services that other Australians had.

These protests condemned the adoption of Aboriginal children by white families.

In the late 1970s the Aboriginal Child Care Agency (ACCA) was established in Victoria and South Australia to help prevent children from being taken away from their families.

In 1980 Link-Up was formed in New South Wales to help children of the stolen generations find their families.

The task of tracing relatives was easier for children who had been in missions and reserves than it was for children who had been adopted. Name changes, inaccurate information, and government laws that prevented adopted children from gaining access to their birth records, made it much more difficult for adopted children to locate their families.

ACCA and Link-Up worked to change the laws that made finding that information hard. They called for a national inquiry into the policy of removal and its effects on those who were taken away and on those who had lost their children.

Over time many of these children were able to trace their families.

They changed our names, they changed our religion, they changed our date of birth, they did all that. That's why today, a lot of them don't know who they are, where they're from. We've got to watch today that brothers aren't marrying sisters; because of the Government. Children were taken from interstate, and they were just put everywhere.

From the *Bringing Them Home* report.

I went to Link-Up who found my family had all died except one sister. I was lucky enough to spend two weeks with her before she died. She told me how my family fretted and cried when I was taken away. They also never gave up of seeing me again.

From the *Bringing Them Home* report.

For those who had thought they were alone, it was a huge surprise to find they had hundreds of relatives. For many it was a time of great joy but also one of immense sadness, loss and anger. Many of those who had been removed came together to support each other.

In the 1980s most State governments accepted that Aboriginal families should be supported to stay together. It was decided that when an Aboriginal child was having trouble at home, he or she should be treated in the same way as other children. In some cases where it was considered necessary for children to be removed from their Aboriginal parents, it was agreed that other relatives or other Aboriginal people should care for them.

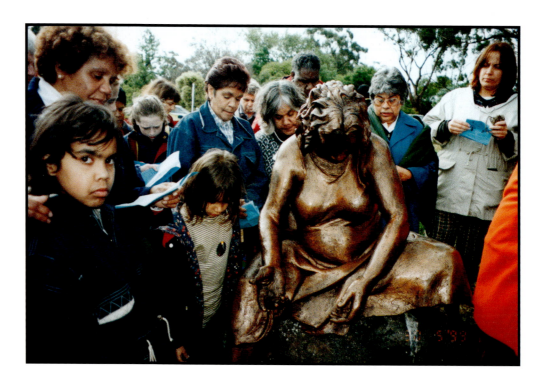

Former residents of Colebrook Home gather with family and friends around the Grieving Mother sculpture at the site of the home in Adelaide.

Bringing Them Home

Between 1995 and 1996 the Human Rights and Equal Opportunity Commission heard evidence from hundreds of Aboriginal people who had been taken away, as well as from some of those who had cared for the children. As a result a written report called *Bringing Them Home* was handed to the Commonwealth parliament on the 26 May 1997.

The report estimated that between 1900 and 1970, between one in three and one in ten Aboriginal children had been removed from their parents. Even though the removal of children was believed at the time to be in the children's best interests, the report found that it had been a failure.

Evidence showed that many of the children grew up with big problems about who they were and why they had been removed.

Some thought they had been abandoned by their parents. Some couldn't love or trust other people in case they were taken away. Others had trouble being parents because they hadn't had real parenting themselves. Many were sad or angry all the time. Some got very sick or hurt themselves. Some drank too much.

It was the government's fault. They didn't do the right thing because they wanted to take the Aboriginal babies away. Some Mums are still looking for their babies but the babies are big people now. They are very sad.

Nick

... the thing is that I just don't trust anybody half the time in my life because I don't know whether they're going to be there one minute or gone the next.

I now understand the way I am and why my life is so full of troubles and fears. I find it hard to take my children to hospital for the fear of being misunderstood and those in authority might take my children away as I was.

From the *Bringing Them Home* report.

The *Bringing Them Home* report, which was released by the Human Rights and Equal Opportunity Commission in 1997, presented evidence from hundreds of members of the stolen generations and those involved with their removal and care.

They wanted to know why their families had been broken up. They wanted to know why they were taken. They wanted someone to say sorry. They wanted help in finding their families. They wanted to find out where they came from. They wanted to be able to learn about their Aboriginal culture and language.

The report showed that it was not their fault that they were taken away. It showed that the government had wanted to stop them growing up as Aboriginal people. It showed that their families were often forced to let them go.

It was very important to the people who were removed as children that the Commission listened to their stories and believed them.

Sorry Day

One of the recommendations of the *Bringing Them Home* report was that all governments and churches involved with the removal of the children should apologise for the harm they had caused.

Since then, all State and Territory parliaments have said they are sorry. The heads of most churches, police, and other organisations that were involved have said they are sorry.

Hundreds of thousands of people have marched in support of the stolen generations. Many thousands have signed their own personal apology.

But so far, the Commonwealth government has refused to apologise.

Each year on the 26 May, lots of people gather together to remember what happened and to talk about what the *Bringing Them Home* report said.

This day is called Sorry Day.

Sorry Day banner designed and created by Adelaide artist, Sally Owen.

33

Journey of Healing

The 1997 *Bringing Them Home* report recommended that there should be help, including counselling, for those affected by child removals. It also recommended that more resources be provided to the Link-Up organisations to assist the stolen generations to find their families and be reunited with them.

In 1999 the Aboriginal people at Uluru (Ayers Rock) invited some of the stolen generations to come to their community.

Each representative was given a set of music sticks to take home to every state.

This was the start of a national Journey of Healing for the children who had been removed, for their families and their communities, and for all of us who share this sad past.

Talking about what has happened, sharing experiences, meeting relatives, crying and laughing, are all part of the Journey of Healing for the stolen generations.

The Journey of Healing music sticks. The fifty-four dots on the lower stick represent the fifty-four recommendations of the *Bringing Them Home* report.

Other Australians can take part in this journey too, by listening to their stories and acknowledging this sad event in our history.

Our journey towards understanding and reconciliation may not be as long or as hard as the journey of Molly, Gracie and Daisy along the rabbit-proof fence.

But if we take the first steps to understand what happened to the stolen children we may ensure that the same thing never happens again.

A Journey of Healing banner painted by Adelaide artists Sally Owen and Tony Shaw and held by Sally and Wiltja school children on Sorry Day 2000.

Time Line

1788
British settlement of Australia. First Fleet arrives at Sydney.

1814
Governor Macquarie opens the "Native Institution" at Parramatta for Aboriginal children. Parents are willing to let their children be fed and attend school but want them to rejoin families later on.

1820
The school closes after all the children have run away.

1839
German missionaries set up a school at Piltawodli on the River Torrens in Adelaide, teaching in the Kaurna language. Other boarding schools follow soon after.

1869
In Victoria Aboriginal girls under 18 and boys under 14 are placed under the control of the Protection Board and can be put into an orphanage or children's home.

1897
The Queensland government makes laws to allow it to separate and remove children from their families.

1901
The Federation of the Commonwealth of Australia is formed. The Federal constitution excludes Aboriginal people from the census and prevents the Commonwealth government from making laws about them. These laws remain with the states.

1905
In Western Australia the Chief Protector is made the guardian of every Aboriginal child under 16 years old.

1909
In New South Wales the government takes control of every child of an Aboriginal person. The Protection Board is given the right to apprentice any Aboriginal child between the ages of 14 and 18 to work for non-Aboriginal people.

1911
The South Australian Aborigines Act gives the government control over almost all aspects of Aboriginal life. Under this Act it becomes illegal for Aboriginal women to mix with non-Aboriginal men. All children, regardless of whether they have parents or relatives, are placed under the guardianship of the Chief Protector until the age of 21.

1931
Molly, Daisy and Gracie follow the rabbit-proof fence from Moore River Settlement to Jigalong.

1937
A national conference on "native welfare" endorses the policy to "assimilate" Aboriginal people of mixed parentage into mainstream society. The control of children and intermarriage is a central part of this policy.

1938
The 150th anniversary of settlement is marked in Sydney by a Day of Mourning organised by the Aborigines' Progressive Association.

1951
State and Commonwealth governments adopt an Assimilation policy that all Aborigines are to become the same as other Australians, and abandon their different cultures and lifestyles.

1967
A referendum amends the Commonwealth constitution to allow the Commonwealth government to make laws affecting Aboriginal people and to count them in the national census.

1976
The Aboriginal Child Care Agency (ACCA) is established in Victoria.

1978
ACCA is set up in South Australia. One year later, a similar organisation, Karu, is founded in Darwin.

1980-88
ACCA is set up in Western Australia and Link-Up is established in New South Wales.

1988
Link-Up commences in Queensland.

1991
The report of the Royal Commission into Aboriginal Deaths in Custody finds that 43 of the 99 people whose deaths were investigated had been removed from their families as children.

1995
The Human Rights and Equal Opportunity Commission (HREOC), chaired by former High Court judge, Sir Ronald Wilson and Aboriginal leader, Mick Dodson, sets up a national inquiry into the separation of Aboriginal children from their families.

1997
The HREOC report, *Bringing Them Home*, is presented to Commonwealth parliament on 26 May.

1998
The First Sorry Day is held on the 26 May.

1999
The Journey of Healing begins at Uluru.

2000
Half a million Australians march across the Sydney Harbour Bridge to show their support for reconciliation and to demand an apology from the Commonwealth government to the stolen generations.

ACKNOWLEDGEMENTS

The author and publisher would like to acknowledge the following individuals and organisations for permission to reproduce the extracts and images in this book.

Front Cover: Kahlin Home, Darwin, 1930s, Eric Wilson Collection, N3636.69. Courtesy of Audiovisual Archives, AIATSIS, Canberra.

Pages 1, 10, 21, 22, 25, 26, 29, 30, 32: Extracts from the report *Bringing Them Home*, 1997. Human Rights and Equal Opportunity Commission, Sydney, www.humanrights.gov.au.

Page 4: A scene from *Rabbit-Proof Fence*. Molly (Everlyn Sampi), Gracie (Laura Monaghan) and Daisy (Tianna Sansbury). Courtesy of Jabal Films Pty Ltd, Jiriki Management, Cameron's Management and the actors, Everlyn Sampi, Laura Monaghan and Tianna Sansbury.

Pages 5, 7, 16, 19, 28, 31: Courtesy of students and staff of St Peter's Lutheran School, Blackwood, South Australia, and SA Link-Up. SA Link-Up is a program of Nunkuwarrin Yunti South Australia Inc, Adelaide.

Page 8: AG290 Watercolour. Artist: Thomas Bock. "Mathinna", 1842. Size 30.2 x 24.9 (irregular). Collection of the Tasmanian Museum and Art Gallery, Hobart.

Page 9: Courtesy of *The Bulletin*, Sydney.

Pages 11 and 12: State Library of SA (SLSA): PRG 1258/2/1995, Point McLeay Mission staff and children, 1885. SLSA: PRG 1258/2/1993, Point McLeay school children, 1880. SLSA: B53023, Classroom at Point McLeay, 1927. SLSA: PRG 1258/2/1967, Young girls skipping at Point McLeay Mission School, 1930. Courtesy of the State Library of South Australia, the Raukkan Council and the Ngarrindjeri Heritage Committee.

Page 13: Toothbrush drill at Point McLeay. Courtesy of the South Australian Museum, the Raukkan Council and the Ngarrindjeri Heritage Committee.

Page 15: NAA: A659, 1940/1/408. Letter headed "Permission to Marry Aboriginals", 1933. Courtesy of the National Archives of Australia, Canberra.

Page 17: (*Top*) GRG 52/45/3/196, State children. Aboriginal child and baby in the arms of a white woman, c. 1911. (*Bottom*) GRG 52/45/3/205, Group of Aboriginal children, c. 1911. Courtesy of State Records of South Australia, Department for Administrative and Information Services, and Department of State Aboriginal Affairs, Government of South Australia.

Page 19: A scene from *Rabbit-Proof Fence*. Molly (Everlyn Sampi), Gracie (Laura Monaghan) and Daisy (Tianna Sansbury) on the way to Moore River Settlement. Courtesy of Jabal Films Pty Ltd, Jiriki Management, Cameron's Management and the actors, Everlyn Sampi, Laura Monaghan and Tianna Sansbury.

Page 20: NAA: F126, Item 33 (dated April1941). Letter from William Bray. Courtesy of Helen Bell, Alice Springs ("To all stolen generations members, so begins the Journey of Healing."), and the National Archives of Australia, Darwin.

Page 23: (*Top*) Meal time at Kahlin "Half-Caste" Home, Darwin, 1930s, Eric Wilson Collection, N3636.71. Courtesy of Audiovisual Archives, AIATSIS, Canberra. (*Bottom*) NAA: A1, 1928/10743. Photo 44. Meal time at the Bungalow, 1928. Courtesy of the National Archives of Australia, Canberra.

Page 24: (*Top*) Croker Island Mission, 1956, AIS photograph. Courtesy of the National Library of Australia, Canberra. (*Bottom*) NAA: A1200, L31997. Aboriginal boys at Kinchela Boys Home, 1959. Courtesy of the National Archives of Australia, Canberra.

Page 25: NAA: A1200, L398025. Adopted children, Retta Dixon Home, c. 1961. Courtesy of the National Archives of Australia, Canberra.

Page 27: (*Top*) Kahlin Home Children, Darwin, 1930s, Eric Wilson Collection, N3636.69. Courtesy of Audiovisual Archives, AIATSIS, Canberra. (*Bottom*) NAA: A1, 1934/6800. Newspaper cutting with handwritten comments. Courtesy of the National Archives of Australia, Canberra.

Page 30: Photo courtesy of Blackwood Reconciliation Group.

Page 32: Front cover of *Bringing Them Home* report. Photography Heide Smith. Courtesy of Heide Smith and Human Rights and Equal Opportunity Commission, Sydney, www.humanrights.gov.au.

Page 33: Image courtesy of Sally Owen, Adelaide.

Page 34: Photo courtesy of Blackwood Reconciliation Group.

Page 35: Photo by Aussie Kanck, Quality Freelancing, Adelaide.

REFERENCES

Bird, Carmel (ed). 1998. *The Stolen Children: Their Stories*. Sydney, Random House.

Haebich, Anna. 2000. *Broken Circles: Fragmenting Indigenous Families 1800-2000*. Fremantle Arts Centre Press.

Human Rights and Equal Opportunity Commission. 1997. *Bringing Them Home: Report of the National Inquiry into the Separation of Aboriginal and Torres Strait Islander Children from Their Families*. Commonwealth of Australia.

Kidd, Rosalind. 2000. *Black Lives, Government Lies*. UNSW Press.

MacDonald, Rowena. 1995. *Between Two Worlds: the Commonwealth Government and the Removal of Aboriginal Children of Part Descent in the Northern Territory*. Alice Springs, IAD Press.

Mattingley, Christobel and Ken Hampton (eds). 1992. *Survival in Our Own Land*. 2nd ed. Sydney, Hodder and Stoughton.

Mellor, Doreen and Anna Haebich (eds). 2002. *Many Voices: Reflections on Experiences of Indigenous Child Separation*. Canberra, National Library of Australia.

Pilkington, Doris. 1996. *Follow the Rabbit-Proof Fence*. Brisbane, University of Queensland Press.

Read, Peter. 1999. *A Rape of the Soul So Profound*. Sydney, Allen and Unwin.